FACILITATION DYNAMICS

Interactive Video Series

INGRID BENS

Participant Guide

Author and Instructional Designer:
  Ingrid Bens, M.Ed., Participative Dynamics

Video Production:
  Jim Amatulli, Amatulli & Associates

Editor:
  Dan Picard, GOAL/QPC

Layout:
  Charles House, Blank Page Design
  Danielle Page, GOAL/QPC
  Michele Kierstead, GOAL/QPC

For information, call or write:

GOAL/QPC
12B Manor Parkway, Salem, NH 03079-2862
Toll free: 800-643-4316
Phone: 603-893-1944
Fax: 603-870-9122
E-mail: service@goalqpc.com
Web site: www.goalqpc.com

Printed in the United States of America.

First Edition
10 9 8 7 6 5 4 3 2
ISBN 1-57681-040-2

Contents

Contents

Contents

Welcome to the Facilitation Dynamics workshop series!

This video series has been created in response to the growing demand for skills in facilitation. Over the past decade, there has been growing recognition that productive meetings happen when proper attention has been paid to the process elements and when the proceedings are skillfully facilitated. Whether you lead a process improvement team, a special project committee, or a departmental work team, meetings need to be run both efficiently and effectively!

The *Facilitation Dynamics* video program is designed to meet the demand for these skills by:

- Providing an overview of the core concepts and techniques of facilitation,
- Creating greater awareness of ineffective practices,
- Providing facilitation tools and techniques that support group effectiveness,
- Encouraging the development of personal facilitation competence.

The program is organized into five modules:

- Module 1: Introduction to Facilitation,
- Module 2: Making Effective Decisions,
- Module 3: Creating Buy-In and Participation,
- Module 4: Managing Group Conflict,
- Module 5: Facilitating Effective Meetings.

In each module, you'll be able to observe facilitation skills in action. You will also be involved in group discussions, practice facilitation exercises, and tackle case studies.

At the end of each module, we hope that you and your team will take some time to talk about how you can use specific tools and techniques to make your next meeting better.

Here are some guidelines to help you get the most from each module:

- Don't be afraid to ask questions; everyone is learning.
- Listen to each other as well as to the workshop leader.
- Plan for follow-up practice sessions so that you can get feedback and reinforcement for your new skills.
- Relax and have fun with these new skills!

Whether you embark on this learning journey alone or in a classroom with others, we're certain that you'll gain valuable strategies and techniques that are relevant to any group interaction.

Your Name _____

Instructor Name _____

Names of Other Participants:

Workshop Schedule:

	Location	Date	Time
Module 1	_____	_____	_____
Module 2	_____	_____	_____
Module 3	_____	_____	_____
Module 4	_____	_____	_____
Module 5	_____	_____	_____

Workshop Guidelines: What norms should we set for ourselves for these workshops?

Facilitation Dynamics

Module 1 Objectives

- Define facilitation and identify the various tools and techniques used in leading an effective group discussion.
- Provide an opportunity to observe facilitation in action.
- Set the stage for further facilitation practice.

Module 1 Workshop Overview

Introduction
- Overview of the workshop objectives.
- Definition of facilitation.
- Core skills practice.

Video
- Introduction to facilitation.
- Demonstration of a facilitator leading a group discussion.

Group Discussion
- Discussion of techniques observed in video segment.

Video
- Summary lecture about core facilitation tools.
- Scenario showing facilitation core techniques.
- Suggestions for follow-up activities.

Closure & Follow-Up Activities
- Identification of future opportunities to practice facilitation skills at upcoming meetings.

Introduction

In many organizations, the idea of using a neutral third party to manage and improve meetings is now taking root. The result is the emergence of a new and important role, in which the person who manages the meeting no longer participates in the discussion or tries to influence the outcome. Instead, he or she stays out of the discussion to focus on how the meeting is being run. Instead of offering opinions, this person provides participants with structure and tools. Instead of promoting a point of view, he or she manages participation to ensure that everyone is being heard. Instead of making decisions and giving orders, he or she supports the participants in identifying their own goals and developing their own action plans.

What is Facilitation?

Facilitation is a way of providing leadership without taking control. The facilitator stays neutral and provides structure so the group can make decisions.

The facilitator's job is to get others to assume responsibility and to take the lead. Rather than being a player, a facilitator's job is to act like a referee, watching the action, more than participating in it. Facilitators control which activities happen but not the decisions reached, and keep their fingers on the pulse of the group to know when to move on or wrap things up.

What Does a Facilitator Do?

Facilitators make their contributions by:
- Helping the group define its overall goal, as well as its specific objectives,
- Helping members assess their needs and create plans to meet them,
- Providing processes that help members use their time efficiently to make high-quality decisions,
- Guiding group discussion to keep it on track,
- Making accurate notes that reflect the ideas of members,
- Helping the group understand its own processes to work more effectively,
- Making sure that assumptions are surfaced and tested,
- Supporting members in assessing their current skills, as well as building new skills,
- Using consensus to help a group make decisions that take all members' opinions into account,
- Supporting members in managing their own interpersonal dynamics,
- Providing feedback to the group so that they can assess their progress and make adjustments,
- Managing conflict using a collaborative approach,
- Helping the group communicate effectively,
- Helping the group access resources from inside and outside the group,
- Creating an environment where members enjoy a positive growing experience,
- Fostering leadership in others by sharing the responsibility for leading the group,
- Teaching and empowering others to facilitate.

What Does a Facilitator Believe?

To be a facilitator, you must firmly believe that:
- People are intelligent, capable, and want to do the right thing,
- Groups can make better decisions than any one person can make alone,
- Everyone's opinion is of equal value, regardless of their rank or position,
- People are more committed to the ideas and plans that they have helped to create,
- Participants can and will act responsibly in assuming true accountability for their decisions,
- Groups can manage their own conflicts and relationships if they are given the right tools and training,
- The process, if well designed and honestly applied, can be trusted to achieve results.

Differentiating Between Process and Content

The two words you'll hear over and over again in facilitation are content (what) and process (how). These are the two dimensions of any interaction between people:

- The **content** of any meeting is *what* is being discussed: the task at hand, the subjects being dealt with, and the problems being solved. The content is expressed in the agenda and the words that are spoken. Because it is the verbal portion of the meeting, the content is obvious and typically consumes the attention of the members.
- **Process** deals with *how* things are being discussed: the methods, procedures, format, and tools used. The process also includes the style of the interaction, the group dynamics, and the climate that is established. Because the process is often silent, it is harder to pinpoint. It is the aspect of most meetings that is largely unseen and often ignored while people are focused on the content.

Content	Process
What	**How**
The subjects for discussion	The methods & procedures
The task	How relations are maintained
The problems being solved	The tools being used
The decisions made	The rules or norms set
The agenda items	The group dynamics
The goals	The climate

The best way to introduce facilitation is to actually practice it. Here are the instructions for this simple warm-up exercise:

1. Find a partner.
2. One of you will be person A. The other one will be person B.
3. You will each take a five-minute turn playing either the role of person A or person B.
4. You will then switch roles for a second five-minute conversation.

Person A plays the content role and shares his or her experience in meetings, describing:

- The things that are currently effective or working well in meetings attended,
- The things that are ineffective about his or her meetings or are not working well,
- What he or she personally wants to learn about facilitation.

Person B plays the process role and acts as a facilitator to Person A by using the five core facilitation tools:

- Staying neutral: not adding thoughts or trying to control the outcome of the conversation,
- Listening actively: facing the speaker, making eye contact, and understanding rather than judging,
- Asking questions: probing, clarifying, and encouraging the other person to say more and dig deeper,
- Paraphrasing key ideas: periodically repeating what the other person is saying to make sure the ideas are being understood,
- Summarizing: giving the speaker a brief, thirty-second summary of what has been said.

Use this space to make notes from the conversation:

What's effective/working	What's not effective/not working

Use this sheet to record any facilitation tools on the video or modeled by your instructor in the classroom.

Actions That Help

___ Listens actively

___ Maintains eye contact

___ Helps identify needs

___ Gets buy-in

___ Surfaces concerns

___ Defines problems

___ Brings everyone into the discussion

___ Uses good body language and intonation

___ Paraphrases continuously

___ Accepts and uses feedback

___ Checks time and pace

___ Provides useful feedback

___ Monitors and adjusts the process

___ Asks relevant, probing questions

___ Keeps an open attitude

___ Stays neutral

___ Offers suggestions

___ Is optimistic and positive

___ Manages conflict well

___ Takes a problem-solving approach

___ Stays focused on process

___ Ping-pongs ideas around

___ Makes accurate notes that reflect the discussion

___ Looks calm and pleasant

___ Is flexible about changing the approach used

___ Skillfully summarizes what is said

___ Knows when to stop

Regardless of the type of discussion being led, all facilitators need to constantly use the core practices:

Stay neutral on content. • Focus on the process role. • Avoid the temptation of offering opinions about the topic under discussion. • Use questions and suggestions to ideas that spring to mind. • Never impose opinions on the group.

Listen actively. • Use attentive body language and paraphrase what group members are saying. • Make eye contact with people while they speak, when paraphrasing what they have just said, and when summarizing their key ideas. • Use eye contact to let people know they can speak next and to prompt quiet people to participate. • Listen to understand, rather than to judge what the speaker is saying.

Ask questions to test assumptions, invite participation, gather information, and probe for root causes. • Use effective questions to delve past symptoms and get at root causes.

Paraphrase to clarify what people say to make sure they know they're being heard, to let others hear their points a second time, and to clarify their key ideas.

Synthesize ideas. • Get people to build on each other's ideas to arrive at collective thinking. • Create consensus and build commitment to decisions.

Stay on track. • Make the group aware if they're off track. The group can then decide to pursue the side track or stop discussion of the new topic and get back to the agenda. • Tape a flipchart sheet to a wall to park off-track items, for placement on a future agenda. • Have a timekeeper to keep discussions on time.

Give feedback. • Telling a group that it's doing well offers encouragement. • If things are not going well, the group members can make needed corrections.

Test assumptions. • Check for underlying thoughts and feelings. • Help the group deal with causes, not just symptoms.

Listen and repeat. • Listen carefully so you can then give a capsule statement that pulls it all together for the members.

Summarize periodically. • Clarifying what is being said can help manage the group and provide focus. • Summaries can be used to revive a discussion that has ground to a halt and bring closure when things are wrapping up.

Use the flipchart so that ideas don't get lost and topics don't need to be repeated. • The notes taken on a flipchart need to be brief, concise, and to the point. • Notes must record what the participants said, not what the facilitator interprets them to have said.

Use the space below to make notes about the various tools and techniques that are described in the second video segment.

Whether you're a facilitator from inside the group or out, the team's leader or a member, the following are parameters for facilitator behaviors:

Be informed. • Always gather information about groups to fully understand their needs.

Be optimistic. • Do not allow disinterest, antagonism, shyness, cynicism, or other negative reactions to throw the group off track. Instead, focus on what can be achieved.

Be consensual. • Facilitation is fundamentally a consensus-building process. Facilitators always strive to create outcomes that reflect the ideas of all participants.

Be flexible. • Always have a process plan for all meetings, yet at the same time, be ready to toss it aside and change direction if that's what is needed.

Be understanding. • Understand that there are a lot of pressures on employees today, and recognize that antagonistic or cynical behaviors are a result of high stress levels.

Be alert. • Become an expert people watcher. Pay careful attention to group dynamics and notice what is going on at all times.

Be firm. • Good facilitation is not a passive activity. It takes assertiveness to keep people on track.

Be unobtrusive. • Do as little talking as possible. Say only enough to give instructions, stop arguments, keep things on track, and sum up.

Facilitating should be an ego-less activity. The purpose is to make the group succeed, not to make yourself the center of attention. An effective facilitator will leave a group convinced that they did it themselves.

Some of the best things that a facilitator can do:

- ❏ Carefully assess the needs of the members,
- ❏ Probe sensitively into people's feelings,
- ❏ Create an open and trusting atmosphere,
- ❏ Help people understand why they are there,
- ❏ Make members the center of attention,
- ❏ Speak in simple and direct language,
- ❏ Work hard to stay neutral,
- ❏ Display energy and appropriate levels of assertiveness,
- ❏ Champion ideas not personally favored,
- ❏ Treat all participants as equals,
- ❏ Stay flexible and ready to change direction if necessary,
- ❏ Make notes that reflect what participants mean,
- ❏ Listen actively to completely understand what is being said,
- ❏ Periodically summarize complex ideas so that they form a coherent summary,
- ❏ Make sure every session ends with clear steps for the next meeting,
- ❏ Ensure that participants feel ownership for what has been achieved,
- ❏ End on a positive and optimistic note.

Some of the worst things a facilitator can do:

- ❏ Remain oblivious to what the group thinks or needs,
- ❏ Never check group concerns,
- ❏ Not listen carefully to what's being said,
- ❏ Lose track of key ideas,
- ❏ Take poor flipchart notes or change the meaning of what is said,
- ❏ Try to be the center of attention,
- ❏ Get defensive,
- ❏ Get into personality battles,
- ❏ Put people down,
- ❏ Allow conflict to rage on,
- ❏ Let a few people dominate,
- ❏ Never check how the meeting is going,
- ❏ Push ahead on an irrelevant agenda,
- ❏ Have no alternative approaches,
- ❏ Let discussions get badly sidetracked,
- ❏ Let discussions end without proper closure,
- ❏ Use inappropriate humor,
- ❏ Not know when to stop.

Take a few minutes to reflect on what you learned in this module.

What surprised you? What had you not realized before today about the role of the facilitator or the way facilitators function?

What seems easy about facilitating?

What seems hard about it? What might you find personally challenging?

What are a few of the specific things you want to learn more about in the rest of this training program?

An excellent way to get better at facilitating is to ask a colleague to observe you in action and then give you feedback. Below is a "Core Practices Observation Sheet" for feedback purposes. Note that this sheet also includes Actions That Hinder so you can identify areas for improvement.

1. Have a colleague observe your facilitation of a group discussion.
2. Sit down in a private place and identify what you think you did effectively.
3. Next, have the observer offer specific descriptions of all the things they noticed that you did effectively.
4. Finally, have the observer provide concrete suggestions for improvements that they believe would enhance your facilitation effectiveness.

Actions That Help

__ Listens actively

__ Maintains eye contact

__ Helps identify needs

__ Gets buy-in

__ Surfaces concerns

__ Defines problems

__ Brings everyone into the discussion

__ Uses good body language and intonation

__ Paraphrases continuously

__ Accepts and uses feedback

__ Checks time and pace

__ Provides useful feedback

__ Monitors and adjusts the process

__ Asks relevant probing questions

__ Keeps an open attitude

__ Stays neutral

__ Offers suggestions

__ Is optimistic and positive

__ Manages conflict well

__ Takes a problem-solving approach

__ Stays focused on process

__ Ping-pongs ideas around

__ Makes accurate notes that reflect the discussion

__ Looks calm and pleasant

__ Is flexible about changing the approach used

__ Skillfully summarizes what is said

__ Knows when to stop

Actions That Hinder

__ Oblivious to group needs

__ No follow-up on concerns

__ Poor listening

__ Strays into content

__ Loses track of key ideas

__ Makes poor notes

__ Ignores conflicts

__ Provides no alternatives for structuring the discussion

__ Puts people down

__ No paraphrasing

__ Let's a few people dominate

__ Never asks "How are we doing?"

__ Tries to be the center of attention

__ Lets the group get sidetracked

__ Projects a poor image

__ Uses negative or sarcastic tone

__ Talks too much

__ Doesn't know when to stop

__ Gets defensive

Facilitation Dynamics

Module 2: Making Effective Decisions

Module 2 Objectives

- Create awareness of common decision-making pitfalls.
- Provide a model of decision-making options and explain when these options are best used.
- Model facilitation strategies during complex decision-making meetings.
- Provide opportunities for facilitation practice and feedback.
- Encourage implementation of better decision-making practices in the workplace.

Module 2 Workshop Overview

Introduction
- Review of the objectives and workshop flow.
- Sharing of reflections on Module 1.
- Assessment of current decision-making practices.
- Facilitation practice.

Video
- Introduction to the importance of making effective decisions.
- Demonstration of a group struggling to make a decision in an unstructured manner.

Group Discussion
- Discussion of observations to analyze what went wrong during the decision-making session.

Video
- Identification of the decision-making pitfalls in the video.
- Review of the six decision-making options.

Case Study
- The "Software Dilemma" group exercise.

Video
- Facilitated decision-making session identifying specific facilitation techniques and answers to the "Software Dilemma" case study.

Group Discussion
- Discussion of tools and strategies to improve decision making at future meetings.

Think about how your work group currently makes decisions.....

What approach or approaches are most commonly used?

TEAM CONCENSUS

EMAIL TEAM FOR TOPIC

MANAGER DICTATES

What are the best things about how your group makes decisions?

TEAM "BUYS" IN

NO SURPRISES

ALL AWARE OF EACH OWN RESPONSIBILITIES

What are the worst aspects? What commonly goes wrong?

ASSIGNED TASK CAN'T PERFORM

NO TIME TO WORK

Name two or three tough decision-making situations you would like to have more strategies for.

Use this sheet to record your observations of the instructor's (or volunteer's) facilitation of the questions on page 20.

Observer's Comments:

Clarifies the purpose

Establishes the process

Checks assumptions

Makes sure there are norms

Creates buy-in if it's needed

Sets time frames

Stays neutral and objective

Paraphrases continuously

Acts lively and positive

Makes clear notes

Asks good probing questions

Makes helpful suggestions

Encourages participation

Maintains a good pace

Periodically checks how it's going

Moves smoothly to new topics

Makes clear and timely summaries

Knows when to stop

Observing a poor decision-making process is sometimes a good starting point. By becoming aware of some of the most common decision-making pitfalls, you can raise your awareness of what **not** to do.

Use the space below to make notes about the shortcomings and flaws you notice in the first video scenario.

_____

_____

_____

_____

_____

_____

_____

_____

_____

_____

_____

Making Effective Decisions

Compare your list of shortcomings with the following:

- No facilitator to play the neutral role,

- No process or decision-making structure,

- Emotional arguing by members,

- Little listening by people with their minds made up,

- Lack of objective exploration of issues and options,

- Lack of clear decision-making criteria for assessing a complex issue,

- Lack of complete information,

- Underutilization of the expertise in the group,

- Aimless and frustrating thrashing through the issues.

Other common mistakes made during decision making include:

- A few people make all the decisions while most others tune out,

- No one keeps track of the time until the whole meeting has been consumed,

- Instead of debating ideas and really listening, people spend their time pushing and pulling to win others over to their view,

- Out of sheer frustration, voting gets overused,

- People "fold" just to get it over with,

- Lack of checking to assess people's degree of commitment to the final decision that's made,

- Conversation simply moves on to another topic when no decision is reached,

- After the meeting is over, people are overheard second-guessing the decision that was made,

- The group fails to create a clear action plan so the same decision has to be discussed all over again at a future meeting.

As a facilitator, you have six distinct decision-making methods available. Each of these options represents a different approach, and each option has pros and cons associated with it.

These six options, in reverse order of their relative value, are:

Option 6: Spontaneous Agreement
This type of decision happens when there is a solution that is favored by everyone and unanimous agreement seems to happen automatically. These types of decisions are usually made quickly, but are fairly rare and often occur in connection with more trivial or simple issues.

Pros: It's fast and easy. Everyone is happy and it unites the group.

Cons: It may be too fast; perhaps the issue actually needed discussion.

Use This Option: When discussion isn't vital or when issues are simple or trivial.

Option 5: One Person Decides
This is a decision option where the group decides to have one person make a decision on behalf of the group. A common misconception among teams is that every decision needs to be made by the whole group. In fact, a one-person decision is often a faster and more efficient way to get resolution. The quality of any one person's decision can be raised considerably if the person making the decision gets input from group members before a decision is reached.

Pros: It's fast and accountability is clear.

Cons: It can divide the group if the person deciding doesn't consult others or makes a decision that others can't live with. A one-person decision typically lacks both the buy-in and synergy that comes from a group decision-making process.

Use This Option: When the issue is unimportant or small, when there's a clear expert in the group, when only one person has the information needed to make the decision and can't share it, or when one person is solely accountable for the outcome.

Option 4: Compromise
Compromise is a negotiated approach used when there are two or more distinct options and neither side is willing to accept the solution/position put forth by the other side. A middle position is then created that incorporates ideas from both sides. Throughout the process of negotiation, everyone wins a few of their favorite points, but also loses a few items they liked. As a result, no one feels they got what they originally wanted, so the emotional reaction is often, "It's not really what I wanted, but I'm going to *have to* live with it."

Pros: It generates a lot of discussion and does create a solution.

Cons: Negotiating when people are pushing a favored point of view tends to be adversarial; hence, this approach divides the group. In the end, everyone wins, but everyone also loses.

Use This Option: When two opposing solutions are proposed, neither of which is acceptable to everyone, or when the group is strongly polarized and compromise is the only alternative.

Option 3: Multi-voting

This priority-setting tool is useful when the group faces a long list of options and rank-ordering them will clarify the best course of action.

Pros: It's systematic, objective, democratic, noncompetitive, and participative. Everyone wins somewhat and feelings of loss are minimal. It's a fast way to sort out a complex set of options.

Cons: There may be limited discussion and therefore, limited understanding of the options. It may force choices on people that may not be satisfactory to them, because the real priorities do not rise to the surface or people are swayed by each other if the voting is done out in the open.

Use This Option: When there is a long list of alternatives or items from which to choose.

Option 2: Majority Voting

Majority voting involves asking people to choose the option they favor, once clear choices have been identified. Usual methods are a show of hands or secret ballot.

Pros: It's fast and decisions can be of high quality if the vote is preceded by thorough discussion.

Cons: It can be too fast and low in quality if people vote based on their personal feelings without the benefit of hearing each other's thoughts. It creates winners and losers, dividing the group. The show of hands method may put pressure on people to conform.

Use This Option: When there are distinct options and one option must be chosen, or when decisions must be made quickly and a division in the group is acceptable.

Option 1: Consensus Building

Creating consensus involves everyone clearly understanding the situation or problem to be decided, analyzing all of the relevant facts together, and then jointly developing solutions that represent the whole group's best thinking about the best outcome for all. It is characterized by a lot of listening, healthy debate, and testing of options. Consensus generates a decision that everyone can live with.

Pros: It's a collaborative effort that unites the group. It creates high involvement. It's systematic, objective, and fact-driven. It builds buy-in and high commitment to the outcome.

Cons: It's time-consuming and produces low-quality decisions if done without proper data collection or if members have poor interpersonal skills.

Use This Option: When decisions will impact the entire group, when buy-in and ideas from all members are essential, or when the importance of the decision being made is worth the time it will take to complete the consensus process properly.

Option	Pros	Cons	Use When
Spontaneous Agreement	• Fast and easy • Unites the group	• May be too fast • Lack of discussion	• Full discussion isn't critical • Issues are trivial
One Person Decides	• Clear accountability • Can be fast	• Lack of input when one person is the expert • No synergy • Low buy-in	• One individual is willing to take responsibility
Compromise	• Encourages discussion • Creates a solution	• Adversarial • Win/lose outcome divides the group	• Positions are polarized and consensus is improbable
Multi-voting	• Systematic • Objective • Participative • Feels like a win	• Limits dialogue • Influenced choices • Real priorities may not surface	• Sorting or prioritizing a long list of options
Majority Voting	• Fast • Creates high quality decisions if dialogue precedes voting • Clear outcome	• May be too fast • Winners and losers • No dialogue • Influenced choices	• Issues are trivial • There are clear options • Division of the group is OK
Consensus Building	• Collaborative • Systematic • Participative • Discussion-oriented • Encourages commitment	• Takes time • Requires data and member skills	• Issues are important • Total buy-in matters • It's important to think creatively

Facilitation Dynamics

All facilitators need to know how important consensus building is. Besides being the number-one choice as a decision-making option for all important decisions, facilitators are constantly building consensus with everything they do.

Examples of consensus building activities include:

- Summarizing a complex set of ideas to the satisfaction of group members,
- Getting everyone's input to create a clear goal and objectives for the group's activities,
- Gaining buy-in from all members to the purpose of the session,
- Linking people's ideas together to align areas of agreement,
- Making notes on a flipchart in such a way that, at the end of the discussion, each member sees where and how he or she has contributed and is satisfied with what has been recorded,
- Discussing and agreeing on which decision-making option to use in a formal decision-making process.

Because all facilitation activities must strive to be collaborative, participative, synergistic, and unifying, all facilitation activities are essentially consensus building in nature!

Hallmarks of the Consensus-Building Process

Regardless of whether consensus is being used formally to reach a decision on a specific issue or informally as an ongoing facilitation technique, the group is working consensually if:

- There are a lot of ideas being shared,
- Discussion is based more on facts than feelings,
- Everyone is heard and people build on each others' ideas,
- There's active listening and paraphrasing to clarify ideas,
- No one is trying to push a predetermined solution,
- When the final solution is reached, people feel satisfied that they were part of the decision,
- Everyone feels consulted and involved so that even though the final solution isn't the one they would have chosen if working independently, they can "live with it."

The essential steps in building consensus are:

1. Creating a joint win/win goal for the activity.
2. Thoroughly analyzing the facts of the situation.
3. Working together to generate a broad range of solutions.
4. Jointly creating criteria, then using these criteria to sort out the best ideas.
5. Creating and implementing action plans.

You should not end a consensus exercise by asking "Is everyone happy?" or even "Does everyone agree?" At the end of even a great consensus process, people have usually made concessions and are likely not getting everything they "wanted."

Consensus isn't designed to make people happy or leave them in 100% agreement. Its goal is to create an outcome that represents the best feasible course of action given the circumstances.

Work alone or with a partner to choose the best decision-making option for each of the following decision-making situations. When you have made your choices, you can discuss them with the entire group or go directly to the video to see how well you did in designing a process for the "Software Dilemma."

C

1. The IT Team needs to make a series of decisions about buying new software for the customer service team. All of the members of the customer service team have strong opinions about the traits of effective software.

cb

There appear to be three software programs that could be purchased. Each package has different strengths and weaknesses. Any decision needs to consider a number of variables such as cost, reliability, simplicity, and degree of available technical support. All of the members of the user group have different needs and concerns.

Which decision-making option should be used for this phase of the decision? Why?

OPD

2. Based on educational background and experience, only one member of the IT Team has the expertise to conduct a thorough assessment of the three software options and determine which most closely meets the priority criteria of the end users.

Which decision-making option should be used for this phase of the decision? Why?

3. Once the final decision about which software program to purchase has been made, the IT Team is faced with two distinct implementation options. Members don't agree on which option they like.

Some think the IT Team should just close for a full week while everyone gets trained at once. This will let them all start working with the new program at the same time. These people argue that the IT Team is operating within a limited time frame and needs to get on with the implementation process.

Other staff members think this is too disruptive and favor staggered training and more gradual implementation over several weeks and even months. These folks think the total change proposal is too drastic.

What decision-making option should be used for this phase of the decision? Why?

4. The marketing department has provided the IT Team with two very different logos to launch their new help line. The members are divided about which logo is best.

Which decision-making option should be used for this phase of the decision? Why?

5. Once the new program is finally about to be rolled out, the IT Team finds that it faces a real challenge booking all of the users into the training sessions using the very limited training room space. In addition, people work in a variety of locations and are operating on different shifts.

Which decision-making option should be used for this phase of the decision? Why?

Use this sheet to record the facilitator techniques demonstrated during the Software Dilemma discussion.

Observer's Comments:

Clarifies the purpose

Establishes the process

Checks assumptions

Makes sure there are norms

Creates buy-in if it's needed

Sets time frames

Stays neutral and objective

Paraphrases continuously

Acts lively and positive

Makes clear notes

Asks good probing questions

Makes helpful suggestions

Encourages participation

Maintains a good pace

Periodically checks how it's going

Moves smoothly to new topics

Makes clear and timely summaries

Knows when to stop

Use the space below to keep track of all the tools and techniques that you noticed the facilitator using in the second video segment. Evaluate these with your colleagues to identify those that are important for implementation by your group.

Tools & Techniques Demonstrated | **Applications for Our Group**

Here are some extra tips to help you manage decision-making sessions.

- Be clear on the process to be used up front. Explain any tools or techniques that will be used.

- Ask people what assumptions they're operating under, either about the issue or the organizational constraints.

- Always handle differences of opinion assertively and collaboratively. Don't avoid conflict or accommodate by pressuring people to get along.

- Urge people not to "fold" just to get things over with. When everyone just gives in, the result is "group think," which creates poor decisions.

- If the group has chosen to go for consensus because the issue is important, stay with it even if the going gets tough. Beware of the tendency to start voting, coin tossing, and bargaining to make things easier.

- Be sure to achieve closure on all major topics. Test for consensus and make sure things are final before letting the group move on to other topics.

- Stop the action if things start "spinning" or behaviors become ineffective. Ask: "What are we doing well?", "What aren't we doing so well?", and "What do we need to do about it?". Then act on the suggestions.

Create Rules or Norms to Guide Your Next Discussion

If a meeting becomes emotional, decision making gets even harder. If you think a topic has the potential to get contentious, it's a wise idea to start the session by asking the members to set a few ground rules. Don't impose these rules; instead ask "norming" questions. For example:

If some people withdraw when the conversation gets tense, the facilitator asks:

> *Sometimes when discussions get intense, only a few people get heard. What can we agree to do at today's meeting to ensure that everyone stays engaged and is really listened to?*

Think about the pitfalls you might encounter at an upcoming tough decision-making meeting. What are three or four questions that the group ought to answer before starting their discussions?

_____

_____

_____

Use this sheet to reflect on what you learned in Module 2.

What had you not realized before this module about the importance of providing process or structure to decision-making discussions?

What are some of the barriers you might expect to encounter when using more structured approaches?

What are some strategies you could use to get people to accept a more systematic approach to decision making?

What new things did you learn about facilitation today from watching the facilitator in the video segment or from the facilitation demonstrations in the classroom?

Facilitation Dynamics

Module 3: Creating Buy-In and Participation

Module 3 Objectives

- Create awareness of the common reasons that people withdraw from active participation.
- Provide a set of high participation techniques and demonstrate how these techniques can be used.
- Model facilitator tools and techniques for getting everyone involved.
- Provide opportunities for facilitation practice and feedback.
- Encourage implementation of buy-in and participation-generation techniques in your meetings.

Module 3 Workshop Overview

Introduction
- Review of the objectives and workshop flow.
- Sharing of insights from Module 2.
- Buy-in exercise for Module 3.

Video
- Scenario showing a meeting in which people withdraw.
- Common reasons people hold back at meetings.
- Identification of factors that contribute to poor participation.
- Prerequisites to ensure participation.

Group Discussion
- Assessment of why people were holding back in the video.

Video
- Demonstration of techniques that create buy-in and build participation.
- Summary lecture about creating participation.

Closure & Follow-Up Activities
- Identification of specific tools and strategies that can be used at future meetings to build buy-in and get active participation.

Think about participation in your typical meeting...

On a scale of 1 to 5, how good is your work group at making sure that all members participate and are heard at meetings?

1	2	3	4	5
We often "lose" people and let a few dominate.		We sometimes are able to get everyone involved.		We always make sure that everyone is fully engaged.

Explain the reasons for the ratings you gave.

What approach or approaches are most commonly used to get ideas from people at your meetings?

Name two or three specific low participation situations for which you would like to have more strategies.

Facilitation Dynamics

As a facilitator, you shouldn't expect that all of your groups will be enthusiastic and engaged. In fact, most groups need considerable warming up and need to learn to use several participation techniques before they'll perform effectively.

As you watch the following video segment, consider these questions for later discussion with your group.

Why did people withdraw? What were their inner concerns?

How did the meeting room contribute to this problem?

How did the leader add to the dilemma? What did he *not* do?

What past events or organizational norms tend to make people hold back?

Your first step in getting people to participate actively is to understand why they often withdraw. Consider the main barriers to participation:

- Members may be confused about the topic being discussed,
- There may be a lack of commitment to the topic under discussion,
- They may feel unsure about the quality of their personal contribution,
- They may be insecure about speaking in front of others,
- They might be afraid of the reaction of their peers,
- Talkative members may "shut down" quieter people,
- Some people may be reluctant to speak up in front of those they consider to be their "superiors,"
- There may be a low level of trust and openness in the group,
- Some traumatic event may have occurred recently that has left some members feeling withdrawn,
- The organization may have a history of not listening to or supporting employee suggestions.

Factors That Affect Participation

When planning any session, it's important to assess how participative the members are likely to be. You can do this before the workshop begins by finding out:

- Whether or not the participants are used to meeting and discussing ideas,
- How the members feel about speaking up in front of their leader and each other,
- Whether relationships between participants are good or strained,
- If there has been a recent layoff, personal tragedy, or other event that might distract participants,
- If members have well-developed group skills such as listening, debating, or decision making,
- How the group has managed past meetings,
- Whether the leader or the organization is likely to support the ideas of the group.

Creating the Conditions for Full Participation

As a facilitator, you need to understand the basic prerequisites for full participation. In general, people will participate fully if they:

- Feel relaxed with the other participants,
- Understand the topic under discussion,
- Have had some say in the planning process,
- Feel committed to the topic,
- Have the information and knowledge needed for fruitful discussion,
- Feel "safe" in expressing their opinions,
- Aren't interfered with or otherwise unduly influenced,
- Trust and have confidence in the facilitator,
- Are comfortable and at ease in the meeting room,
- Feel that the organization will support their ideas.

As you view the second meeting on the video, please identify:

What did the leader say or do to get participation and buy-in?	How can we use this in our meetings?

Facilitation Dynamics

© 2001 GOAL/QPC

Use this sheet to record your observations of the discussion on page 42.

Observer's Comments:

Clarifies the purpose

Establishes the process

Checks assumptions

Makes sure there are norms

Creates buy-in if it's needed

Sets time frames

Stays neutral and objective

Paraphrases continuously

Acts lively and positive

Makes clear notes

Asks good probing questions

Makes helpful suggestions

Encourages participation

Maintains a good pace

Periodically checks how it's going

Moves smoothly to new topics

Makes clear and timely summaries

Knows when to stop

People may not automatically be enthusiastic to participate. It's important to determine how many of the following realities are factors that may affect participation:

- People are working extra hours and don't know how they'll find the time for meetings,
- Facilitated meetings usually generate many action plans, creating extra work that no one wants,
- The organization may not support the ideas generated by employees; organizational priorities could shift tomorrow,
- There may be a feeling that the improvements gained will only benefit the organization, not the individuals involved.

It's foolish to attempt to run any meeting without gaining commitment and buy-in from the participants. Getting people to commit is achieved by asking them to answer the buy-in question, "What's in it for me?"

An effective buy-in activity is to pair up participants at the start of any session and ask them to spend five minutes discussing two questions:

> *What is the gain for the organization in solving this problem or fixing this process?*

> *How will I personally benefit if we solve this problem or fix this process?*

After the discussion, participants can recount their own or their partner's responses. Identify reasons for not participating that you'll need to spend more time on, and record all comments on the flipcharts.

The participants' responses to question 2 amount to their psychological buy-in to the session. In cases of heightened levels of resistance, questions can be added to the partner buy-in exercise:

> *What is blocking me personally from participating? Why might I be reluctant?*

> *What will it take to overcome these blocks? Under what conditions and with what support will I consider giving this my full attention?*

When you record members' responses to these additional questions, you will, in effect, be negotiating their participation.

People may say they'll participate if there are assurances from senior management for support of their ideas or they might ask for assurances that the decisions made will be honored. They might ask to be given time off, help, or other compensation for their added efforts. Having their conditions on the table lets you assess the extent to which the participants are feeling blocked.

Think about an upcoming meeting in your organization. Accept that some people may be less than thrilled to be there. What buy-in question could you ask to help them identify "what's in it for them?"

Here are some techniques to get reluctant participants to play an active role in meetings.

1. Discussion Partners

One way to start any discussion is to pose a question to a large group, then ask everyone to find a partner to discuss the question for a few minutes. When the allotted time is up, have people report on what they discussed.

2. Tossed Salad

Place an empty cardboard box or an inexpensive plastic salad bowl on the table. Distribute small slips of paper and ask people to write down one good idea per slip. Put the slips into the bowl or box and have someone "toss the salad." Pass the salad around so that each person can take out as many slips as he or she tossed in. Go around the table and have people share ideas. Discuss and refine the most promising comments.

3. Issues and Answers

When faced with a long list of issues, put each issue on a separate sheet of flipchart paper and post the sheets around the room. (This technique works best as a stand-up activity.) Have people go to one of the issue sheets and discuss that problem with whomever else was drawn to that sheet. Make sure people are distributed evenly, with at least three people per issue. Allow up to five minutes for the subgroups to analyze the situation and have them make notes on the top half of the flipchart sheet. Ask everyone to move to another flipchart sheet and read the analysis made by the first group, adding additional ideas. Keep moving people around until everyone is back at their original sheet. Ask everyone to generate and record solutions to their respective issue on the bottom half of the sheet. Once again, circulate people until everyone has added ideas to all of the sheets. To end the process, have everyone walk by each sheet, read the solutions, and check off the one or two ideas they think are the best. When everyone is seated, review the ideas. Ask small groups to each take responsibility for creating action plans for the ideas on one of the sheets.

4. Talk Circuit

Start by posing a question to the group. Allow quiet time for each person to write their own response. Ask everyone to sit "knee to knee" with a partner and share their ideas. Have one person speak while the other acts as the facilitator. After two to three minutes, have partners reverse their roles. After an additional two or three minutes, stop the discussions. Ask everyone to find a new partner and repeat the process. Repeat this exercise as many times as desired, then discuss the ideas with the whole group and record them on flipcharts.

5. Pass the Envelope

Give each person an envelope filled with blank slips of paper. Pose a question or challenge to the group, and have everyone write down as many ideas as they can within a given time frame. Put the slips into the envelopes and tell people to pass the envelopes, either to the next person or in all directions. When the passing stops, have the participants read the contents. Pair off participants and have them discuss the positives and negatives of each idea. Ask them what other ideas they could add. Combine pairs to form groups of four and ask them to further refine the content of their four envelopes into practical action plans. Finally, hold a plenary to collect ideas.

Use this page to reflect on the facilitation tools and techniques shared in Module 3.

What further insights did you gain from the facilitation tools and techniques in the video?

What new things did you learn about facilitation from watching people practice in the classroom?

What additional skills are you now realizing that you need to gain to become a more proficient facilitator?

Facilitation Dynamics

Module 4 Objectives

- Create awareness of the elements of a dysfunctional meeting.
- Provide a format for making immediate interventions.
- Model facilitator tools and techniques for dealing assertively with conflict in a group.
- Provide opportunities for facilitation practice and feedback.
- Encourage implementation of new norms and strategies to reduce or handle problems with work groups in the workplace.

Module 4 Workshop Overview

Introduction
- Review of workshop objectives and agenda.
- Discussion of insights from Module 3 and learning needs of group members.
- Exploration of current conflict patterns.
- Differentiating between debates and arguments.

Video
- Demonstration of a group meeting in which tempers rise as conflicts emerge.

Group Discussion
- Identification of the factors that contributed to the downward spiral of the ineffective meeting.

Video
- Analysis of what went wrong with the first meeting for comparison with your group's observations.
- Lecture on how facilitators make interventions when group behaviors decline.

Group Exercise
- Presentation of the three-step intervention wording model.
- Intervention wording exercise.

Video
- Facilitated conflict scenario showing interventions.

Group Discussion
- Discussion of the intervention techniques used in the video.

Closure & Follow-Up Activities
- Summary lecture about facilitator strategies for dealing with conflict.
- Discussion of ideas for dealing with conflict at future meetings.

Think about your experience in past meetings…

On a scale of 1 to 5, describe the tendency for your work group to get embroiled in a conflict that becomes dysfunctional.

1	2	3	4	5
We often end up embroiled in arguments that become bogged down and emotional.		We sometimes end up in dysfunctional arguments.		We usually engage in healthy debates.

Describe what happens.

Name two or three specific conflict situations for which you would like to gain facilitation strategies.

Dealing with conflict is a fact of every facilitator's life. Accept that conflict is inevitable, and be prepared to deal with it!

Consider the following scenario: Imagine yourself facilitating an important meeting. Everything is going along great until you reach the third agenda item. Suddenly two members start arguing. Listening goes out the window, as each person pushes his or her ideas. The rest of the group gets uncomfortable as the two combatants become more and more emotional. The discussion spins in circles and people get upset!

What do you do now? For starters, rather than seeing conflict as a disaster, you need to view conflict as a positive sign that people care about the issue and have energy to put toward solutions. What determines whether conflict deteriorates into a disaster or leads to a useful debate is how it's handled.

Differentiating Between Debates and Arguments

All facilitators need to be attuned to the differences between a debate and an argument. Healthy debate is essential. If a group doesn't express differences of opinion, it will be incapable of making effective decisions.

In Healthy Debates	In Dysfunctional Arguments
People are open to hearing other's ideas.	People assume they're right.
People listen and respond to ideas even if they don't agree with them.	People wait until others have finished talking, then state their ideas without responding to the ideas of the other person.
Everyone tries to understand the views of the other person.	No one is interested in how other people see the situation.
People stay objective and focus on the facts.	People get personally attacked and blamed.
There's a systematic approach to analyzing the situation and looking for solutions.	Hot topics get thrashed out in an unstructured way.

As you watch the struggles of this next group, see if you can identify all of the things that contribute to the collapse of this meeting.

Your notes	**Narrator comments**

During any meeting, there are occasions when the facilitator may need to make an intervention. An intervention is any action or set of actions deliberately taken to improve the functioning of the group. This may be necessary in situations when:

- Someone isn't listening or has dropped out of the conversation,
- Two people are having a side conversation that is distracting to others,
- People are interrupting each other and not understanding key ideas,
- One person uses a sarcastic or otherwise inappropriate tone during a debate,
- Comments get personal,
- The discussion goes off track.

Intervening is like holding up a mirror to the participants so that they can see what they're doing and take steps to correct the problem. An intervention is always an interruption. It stops the group's discussion about the content and draws members' attention to the process. The aim is always to resolve the problem as quickly as possible so that the members can return to their task.

The need to intervene may arise because of one individual or it may be interpersonal, involving a conflict between two or more people. Groups can also experience problems that involve all of the members.

Deciding Whether or Not to Intervene

As a facilitator, you always need to be cautious when deciding whether or not to intervene. If you intervened every time there was a problem, you might be interrupting too frequently. Instead, you need to keep a watchful eye for repetitive, inappropriate behaviors that don't seem to resolve themselves. Ask yourself:

- Is the problem serious?
- How much time will intervening take? Do we have that time?
- How much of a disruption will intervening cause?
- How will it impact relationships or the flow of the meeting?
- Can the intervention hurt the climate?
- Will it damage anyone's self-esteem?
- What is the chance that the intervention will work or fail?
- Do I know these people well enough to do this?
- Do I have enough credibility to do this?
- Is it appropriate, given their level of openness and trust?

Finally, a good question to ask yourself is, "What will happen if I do nothing?" If the answer is that the group will be less effective if you do nothing, you're obligated to take action.

Interventions are always risky because they can make any situation worse. For this reason, interventions need to be worded carefully. There are generally three distinct components to an intervention statement:

Step 1: *Describe what you see.* This description is nonjudgmental and doesn't attribute motive. It is based solely on observations of actual events. (i.e., "Allen and Sue, both of you have left and returned three times during this meeting.")

Step 2: *Make an impact statement.* Tell members how their actions are impacting you, the process, or other people. Base this on actual observations. (i.e., "We had to stop our discussion and start over three times.")

Step 3: *Redirect the person's behavior(s).* This can be done by either:

(a) Asking members for their suggestions about what to do. (i.e., "What can you do to make sure this doesn't happen again?")

or

(b) Telling members what to do. (i.e., "Please either leave or stay for the rest of the meeting.")

An impact statement (step 2) can be omitted from an intervention if it feels like it's laying excessive guilt on the offending parties. You need to use your judgment as to whether or not the situation requires a focus on "impact." A good rule of thumb is to use impact statements when the offensive behavior is persistent or repetitive and previous intervention attempts have been ignored.

Of the three steps, the most important is step 3, the redirect. Many effective interventions consist only of offering the redirect. (i.e., "I need everyone to give the meeting their full attention.")

Common Intervention Language

Because the wording of interventions is so important, here are some sentences and sentence stems that are commonly used:

"I'd like to describe what I am seeing here and get your reaction to it."

"I'm noticing that . . ."

"I'm concerned that..."

"A pattern I have observed is..."

"I'd like to offer this observation."

"It strikes me that..."

"Let's stop for a moment and look at what's happening here."

"What are people experiencing right now?"

"How do people feel that things have gone thus far?"

When people start to get emotional, there are specific responses that can effectively redirect negative behavior in different situations. You will notice that none of these redirecting statements puts down the person or is in any way critical. All offer the other person a chance to save face and to say or do the right thing.

When someone is being sarcastic:

"Ellen, I'm afraid your good ideas aren't being heard because of the tone of voice you're using. How about stating that again, only in a more neutral way?"

When one person is putting down the ideas of another:

"Joe, I'm concerned you're not hearing the ideas Carol is putting on the table. I'm going to ask you to explore these ideas by asking a few questions to make sure you fully understand them before dismissing them. It will make Carol feel more like she's being heard."

When two people are arguing, cutting each other off, and not listening to each other:

"I'm afraid neither of you are hearing the excellent points being made by the other. I'm going to ask you both to first paraphrase what the other has said before you make your own comment."

When someone is inappropriately aggressive or hurtful to another person:

"Fred, I'm going to stop you from saying anything further for just a moment and ask June to tell you how she needs to have you interact with her during the rest of this meeting. June, what would be a better way of interacting?"

When one person dominates the discussion:

"Al, you always have a lot of valuable ideas, but we need to hear from the other members of the team. Would you please hold your comments until the end so that other people can express their ideas?"

When someone has hurled a personal slur at someone else:

"Jim, rather than characterizing Sally as being 'sloppy,' please tell her specifically about the state of the meeting room after her session, so that she can address the situation."

When two people are trashing each other's ideas without giving them a fair hearing:

> "You are discounting each other's ideas very quickly. I'm going to ask that you give a quick recap of what the other person said before launching into your own points."

When a person makes only negative remarks about the ideas of another person:

> "Mary, what do you like about what Chuck just said?"

When people run in and out of a meeting:

> "In the last ten minutes, three people have gone in and out of this meeting, disrupting the discussion. What should be done about this?"

When everyone has fallen silent:

> "Everyone has become pretty quiet in the last few minutes and we haven't had any new ideas. What can we do to get things going again?"

When the whole group is acting dysfunctional:

> "I'm going to stop this discussion. I'm noticing that two people are talking among themselves while three others are arguing emotionally. What can we do to make the rest of this meeting run more smoothly?"

When members are disregarding their previously set norms:

> "I'm going to suggest we stop this meeting for a few minutes to look back at the norms we set last week. Are we following them? Do we need to add a few new ones?"

When the meeting has totally digressed:

> "I need to point out that we have now digressed and are onto another topic. Is this the topic the team wants to discuss or should we park it and go back to the original agenda item?"

Telling Versus Asking

In some of the preceding interventions, the facilitator told people what to do, while in others they were asked. Still in others, it sounded like the facilitator was only making a suggestion.

When you intervene, you need to make a judgment about which of these approaches to use, situation by situation. While there are no hard and fast rules, here are some guidelines:

- Asking is always better than telling because people are more likely to accept their own intervention,
- It's always appropriate for facilitators to suggest or tell people what to do on matters of process,
- A directive or telling response is appropriate if the individuals are exhibiting extremely dysfunctional behavior,
- The more a group acts maturely and responsible, the more effective it is to ask rather than tell.

Practice your intervention skills by identifying the exact wording you would use if you had to correct each of the following situations. Remember to use the three-step intervention wording model as a guide.

1. Al has a lot of good ideas; too many in fact. He tends to dominate and talk way too much. He's just about to launch into yet another long speech. What is the effective thing to say to Al?

2. Ellen and Fred are beginning to get emotional and repeat the same points over and over. You are sure that neither of them is really listening to the other. What is the effective thing to say to Ellen and Fred?

3. Chuck is giving a very critical review of Mary's program. Mary has now fallen silent and is looking hurt. What is the effective thing to say to Chuck?

4. The meeting has been going very well but now the whole group has fallen silent. Some people are looking through their planners. Others are just slumped in their seats, looking dazed. What is the effective thing to say to the whole group?

Meeting Observation Sheet

As you watch the facilitated conflict scenario, make notes about the dysfunctions you notice and the specific actions or interventions the facilitator uses to deal with each one. When your list is complete, work with others to create a shared set of observations.

Dysfunctions Noticed	Specific Facilitator Actions Taken

Use this sheet to record your observations of the facilitator leading the discussion from page 59.

Observer's Comments:

Clarifies the purpose

Establishes the process

Checks assumptions

Makes sure there are norms

Creates buy-in if it's needed

Sets time frames

Stays neutral and objective

Paraphrases continuously

Acts lively and positive

Makes clear notes

Asks good probing questions

Makes helpful suggestions

Encourages participation

Maintains a good pace

Periodically checks how it's going

Moves smoothly to new topics

Makes clear and timely summaries

Knows when to stop

It's the job of the facilitator to handle negative emotions so that they don't poison the dynamics of the group. Here are some basic strategies you can use:

Slow things down: Get the attention of the group; interrupt if necessary and ask others to slow down. Get people to repeat their key ideas.

Stay totally neutral: Never take sides or allow your body language to hint that you favor one idea over another. If you appear to favor one opinion over another, you will have lost your ability to mediate.

Stay calm: Maintain your composure and do not raise your voice. Speak slowly and with an even tone. Avoid emotional body language.

Revisit the norms: Point them out and remind people that they agreed to them earlier on. Make needed additions to the norms.

Be assertive: Get into "referee mode." Enforce that people speak one at a time. Have them raise their hands. Don't hesitate to stop people who interrupt. Don't stand by passively while people fight.

Make interventions: Don't let people fight with each other or display rudeness. Learn and use the appropriate wording for different situations.

Emphasize listening: Paraphrase key points and ask others to do the same thing any time you sense they aren't really hearing each other.

Call time-out: Don't hesitate to stop the action if emotions get out of hand or if the discussion is spinning in circles. Ask, "Are we making progress?" "Are we using the right approach?" "How are people feeling?" Implement their suggestions for improving the meeting. If they have none, offer ideas for improvement.

Use a structured approach: Have a technique in mind and use it. This can be forcefield analysis, multi-voting, systematic problem solving, a decision grid, cause and effect analysis, or any of a number of others. Never lead a discussion without identifying the process.

Use the flipchart: Make notes of key points so they aren't lost and the group won't be forced to go over the whole thing again. Read back the notes on the flipchart any time you want to get regain center stage.

Create closure: Make sure that the discussion isn't in vain by helping the members create a clear summary of what has been agreed. If applicable, help the group create action plans to ensure implementation of key suggestions.

To get maximum benefit from this module, reflect on the dysfunctions you see in your own group and identify strategies that could be applied that will make future meetings more effective. Try to think of at least one improvement for each of your current problems.

Things we're doing now that limit our effectiveness	Ideas for improvement/new norms or strategies we need

Take a few minutes to reflect on managing group conflict.

What surprised you? What had you not realized before today about the role of the facilitator in a conflict situation?

What do you expect will be difficult about assertively managing inappropriate behavior? What can you do to overcome these blocks?

What are a few of the specific things you still feel you need to learn about facilitation during the last module of this training program?

Facilitation Dynamics

Module 5 Objectives

- Create awareness of the elements of effective and ineffective meetings.
- Provide a structure for organizing meeting components.
- Model strategies for balancing the roles of facilitator and chairperson.
- Provide opportunities for facilitation practice and feedback.
- Encourage implementation of more structure into your work group's next meeting.

Module 5 Workshop Overview

Introduction
- Review of the objectives and workshop flow.
- Sharing of insights from Module 4 and discussion of the effectiveness of current meetings.
- Exploration of the common elements of effective and ineffective meetings.

Video
- Identification of what makes meetings effective and ineffective.
- Case study showing the "Team in Overtime" having an ineffective meeting.

Group Discussion
- Group assessment of what went wrong in the video meeting.
- Identification of remedies to repair the case scenario meeting.
- Creation of a revised meeting agenda.

Video
- Demonstration of effective facilitation and answers to the case study.
- The importance of process and structure.

Group Discussion
- Redesign of future meeting agendas to incorporate tools and techniques.

Closure & Follow-Up Activities
- Review of applications for facilitation.
- Evaluation and planning of continuous learning activities.

Think about the overall quality of your current meetings...

On a scale of 1 to 5, describe the organization and effectiveness of your work group meetings.

1	2	3	4	5
Poor	Fair	Satisfactory	Good	Excellent

Explain the reasons for the ratings you gave.

Identify the three most important problems that your work team should address to improve this rating.

Identify two or three things that you would like to learn about facilitation during this module.

Common Elements of Ineffective Meetings

As facilitator, it's your job to help others learn how to work effectively to achieve their goals.

Some common elements of ineffective meetings include:

- Lack of clarity about the meeting goal,
- A vague or nonexistent agenda,
- No time limits on discussions,
- No discernible process for working on important issues,
- No facilitation of discussions,
- People haven't done their homework,
- Discussions go in circles,
- Lack of closure to discussions,
- People vehemently arguing points of view rather than debating ideas,
- A few people dominating while others sit passively,
- Meetings that end without detailed action plans for agreed-to next steps,
- Absence of any process checking of the meeting as it unfolds, or any evaluation at the end,
- Too many meetings.

Common Elements of Effective Meetings

By contrast, here are the ingredients shared by all effective meetings:

- A detailed agenda that spells out what will be discussed, the goal of the discussion, who is bringing that item forward, and an estimate of how long each item will take,
- Clear process notes that describe the tools and techniques that will be used,
- Assigned roles such as facilitator, chairperson, minute taker, and timekeeper,
- A set of group norms created by the members and posted in the meeting room,
- Clarity about decision-making options and how they will be used,
- Effective member behaviors,
- Periodic process checks to make sure progress is being made,
- Clear conflict management strategies,
- A process that creates true closure,
- Detailed and clear minutes,
- Specific follow-up plans,
- A post-meeting evaluation.

As you watch the ineffective meeting scenario unfold in the video, make notes about what you notice to be wrong.

A Team in Overtime

The Shipping and Receiving Team has been holding marathon meetings lately. Instead of the scheduled two hours, they've been meeting for over three hours. The worst part is nothing much gets done! People are beginning to think the whole team thing is a huge waste of time.

Because the meetings take so long, members run in and out. At the last meeting, the leader read memos and let people share information for over an hour and a half. During much of this time, three of the team's members just sat and listened to information they had already received from the team leader.

The team then started to discuss a major problem with suppliers, but ran out of time. This was an unstructured discussion that no one facilitated, and during which several people got quite heated with each other. Unfortunately the discussion never reached a conclusion that anyone would describe as a clear consensus. The remainder of the discussion was therefore put onto the agenda for the next meeting. This delay frustrated a lot of people because they felt that such an important problem needed to be resolved that day.

While people were gathering their things to leave, the decision to order new software for the automatic reorder process was more or less announced. While this was a rather contentious issue about which some team members had serious reservations, the decision to proceed was justified by announcing that time didn't permit any further discussion or delays. Because one of the members had been delegated responsibility for researching software options, the other members felt reluctant to question her authority.

A few new items were quickly added onto the agenda for next time and members hurried off to get back to their jobs. There was no evaluation of how the meeting had gone, but people had a lot of complaints when they got back to their desks!

Based on your notes from the "Team in Overtime" case study, work with other participants to develop a complete list of what was wrong and also what you collectively think are the remedies for this situation.

What was missing or wrong with this meeting?	What would you do to fix it?

Use this sheet to record your observations of the facilitator leading the analysis of the ineffective meeting.

Observer's Comments:

Clarifies the purpose

Establishes the process

Checks assumptions

Makes sure there are norms

Creates buy-in if it's needed

Sets time frames

Stays neutral and objective

Paraphrases continuously

Acts lively and positive

Makes clear notes

Asks good probing questions

Makes helpful suggestions

Encourages participation

Maintains a good pace

Periodically checks how it's going

Moves smoothly to new topics

Makes clear and timely summaries

Knows when to stop

Below are some of the symptoms of dysfunctional meetings and prescriptions for their cure. If you help team members become aware of their patterns, they can begin to adjust them.

SYMPTOMS	CURES
As each person finishes speaking, the next person starts a new topic. There is no building on ideas, thus no continuity of discussion. This results in a half-dozen topics in the air.	Have each person acknowledge the comments of the last speaker. Make it a rule to finish a point before moving forward.
People argue their side, trying to convince others that they're right rather than understanding either the issue or anyone else's input. There is no listening.	Train members to paraphrase what is said in response to their point. Use the flipchart to record all sides of an issue. Try to reach a decision only after getting everyone to understand the differing views.
As soon as a problem is mentioned, someone announces that they understand the problem. A solution is quickly proposed and the discussion moves to another topic.	Use cause and effect diagrams or systematic problem solving to bring structure to meetings. Become thorough in solving problems. Avoid jumping to obvious solutions.
Whenever someone disagrees with a group decision, the dissenting view is ignored.	Develop an ear for dissenting views and make sure they get heard. Have someone paraphrase the dissenting opinion.
The group uses brainstorming and voting to reach all decisions.	Preplan meeting processes so other tools are on hand, and then use them.
Conversations often go nowhere for twenty to thirty minutes. In frustration, the group goes on to another topic.	Set a time limit on each discussion and halfway through, evaluate how it's going. Use periodic summaries and push for closure.
People often speak in an emotional tone of voice. Sometimes they even say things to others that are quite personal.	Have people stop and rephrase their comments so there are no distracting personal innuendoes.
Group members hold frequent side meetings to discuss what they're thinking. No one says any of this to the entire group.	Encourage honesty by valuing all input. Draw side chatterers back to the general conversation.
Group members don't notice they've become sidetracked on an issue until they've been off-topic for quite awhile.	Have a signal to flag off-track discussions. Decide if you want to digress or park the particular issue.
The real extroverts or those with "power" do most of the talking. Some team members say very little at meetings.	Use round-robins to get input. Call on members by name. Use idea slips to get written comments from everyone.
No one pays attention to body language or notices that some people have tuned out or even seem agitated.	Make perception checks and ask people to express their feelings.
There is no closure to most topics. Little action takes place between meetings.	Stress closure. Reach a clear decision and record it. Bring actions forward at the next meeting.
There is little achieved week after week.	Evaluate meetings and discuss the outcome before the next meeting. Post any new rules or improvement ideas.

1. Create and use a detailed agenda.

Each meeting must have an agenda that's been developed ahead of time and ratified by the members of the team. This lets members come to the meeting prepared to make decisions.

A detailed agenda should include:
- Topics for discussion, plus a brief description of what is involved and what needs to be accomplished,
- A time guideline for each item,
- The name of the person bringing the item forward,
- The details of the process to be used for each discussion.

If the agenda can't be designed in advance, then the first order of business at the meeting must be a facilitated discussion in which members design the agenda for that day's session.

2. Develop step-by-step process notes.

Most of the books that have been written on meetings don't mention process notes, largely because these books are geared toward meetings that will be chaired rather than facilitated. When a meeting is facilitated, you will need detailed process notes for each agenda item. These notes specify the tools and techniques to be used, and how participation will be managed.

In the sample agenda on the next page, we've added process notes to illustrate their important role.

Sample Agenda with Process Notes

Name of Group: Customer Fulfillment Team
Members: Jane, Mohammed, Jacques, Elaine, Carl, Fred, Diane, Joe
Meeting Details: Monday, June 12, 1999, 11:00 a.m. to 1:00 p.m.,
       Conference Room C

Agenda Items (What & Why)	Process Notes (How)
Warm up (10 min.) - Joe • To create focus	• Have team members share one recent customer contact story.
Review agenda and norms (5 min.) - Joe • To set context	• Ratify the agenda and norms through general discussion. Add any new items and make sure there is clarity about the overall goal of the meeting.
Bring forward action items (25 min.) - Entire group • To monitor implementation	• Have members briefly report back on action plans created at the last meeting. Add any new plans.
Focus group updates (20 min.) - Jacques & Diane • To identify areas for improvement	• Report on the outcomes of six customer focus groups. Use forcefield analysis to distinguish between what we are doing well and what we aren't.
Prioritize customer issues (20 min.) - Joe • To set priorities	• Establish criteria to evaluate customer concerns. Use criteria matrix to appraise each issue and determine top priorities for action.
Problem-solve priority issues (30 min.) - Entire group • To create improvement plans	• Divide into two sub-teams to problem-solve the top two priority issues. Create detailed action plans for the top issues, then meet as a group to share and ratify ideas.
Next-step planning and agenda building (10 min.) - Joe • To ensure closure and design the next session	• Make sure everyone knows what they're expected to work on. Start to form an agenda for the next meeting.
Exit survey (10 min.) - Joe • To check meeting effectiveness	• Have everyone evaluate the meeting on their way out the door. Bring this information forward at the next meeting.

3. Clarify roles and responsibilities.

Effective meetings require people to play defined roles, including:

- Facilitator: Designs the methodology for the meeting, manages participation, offers useful tools, helps the group determine its needs, keeps things on track, and periodically checks on how things are going.

- Chairperson: Runs the meeting according to defined rules, but also offers opinions and engages in the discussion if he or she chooses. The chairperson has traditionally not been neutral. Most often, the chairperson of any meeting is the official leader, who plays an active role as decision maker and "opinion leader."

- Minute taker: Takes brief, accurate notes of what is discussed and the decisions made. Also responsible for incorporating the notes on flipcharts.

- Timekeeper: Keeps track of the time and reminds the group periodically if they're staying within guidelines. The role of timekeeper often rotates among members.

- Scribe: Writes/records comments on a flipchart. Some facilitators are more comfortable asking others to make notes on the flipchart while they facilitate. This has the benefit of freeing the facilitator from the distractions of writing, but adds its own complications. The scribe may start facilitating or may not make the notes the way the facilitator wants. Having a scribe takes a lot of coordination.

Balancing the Roles of Chairperson and Facilitator

Chairing and facilitating are two distinct meeting management roles. Each has its strengths and its place.

- Chairing is most useful at the start of a meeting to go over minutes, share information, and manage a round-robin report-back by members. Chairing traditionally relies on the use of Parliamentary Rules of Order. Because chairs are not neutral, one major drawback is that they tend to influence decisions and concentrate power. It's not uncommon for a strong chairperson to make final decisions on important items.

- Facilitating is designed to foster participation when the input of all members is needed to decide issues. Facilitators use a structured approach to encourage consensus and collaboration to reach important decisions. Facilitation creates rules from within the group, rather than imposing rules from a book.

It's common to have a meeting leader who uses a chairperson approach to start the meeting and take care of the housekeeping and information-sharing portions of the session, and then switches to facilitation to get input on the discussion topics within the agenda.

All good facilitators should know when and how to act as an effective chairperson. Conversely, it would be ideal if all chairpersons were also skilled facilitators, who could switch styles when they wanted to get participation and ownership.

With some planning beforehand, these roles don't need to clash. The key is to remember that each has its place.

In summary:

Chair when you want to:

- Review past minutes and agenda items,
- Exchange information,
- Hear members report back,
- Discuss next steps.

Facilitate when you want to:

- Increase participation,
- Shift ownership,
- Get members to make decisions,
- Get members to create action plans.

4. Set clear meeting norms.
Make sure that the group has clear norms for behavior and that those norms are created by the group.

5. Manage participation.
Make sure that everyone is part of the discussion, that structure exists for each item, and that there is an effective use of decision-making tools to bring closure to all items.

6. Make periodic process checks.
Process checking is a technique that every facilitator should utilize during meetings to keep meetings from going off track. It involves stopping the discussion and turning the group's attention to how the meeting is going.

There are four things you can check:

- Progress: Ask members if they think the goals are being achieved. Are problems being solved? Are decisions being made? Check the meeting progress if things seem to be getting stuck, at points of closure, and at least once per session.

- Pace: Check the pace when things seem to be dragging or moving too fast, any time people look frustrated, and at least once per session or meeting. Ask if things are moving too quickly or too slowly. Get any suggestions for improving the pace, and implement these immediately.

- Process: Check the process being used in the meeting when the tool the group is using isn't yielding the results you hoped for, or when it's evident that the process isn't being followed as laid out. Ask members if the tool or approach being used is working or needs to be changed. Ask for or offer suggestions for another approach.

- Pulse: Check the "pulse" of the meeting any time members look distracted, tired, or frustrated, and at least once during each session. Ask members how they're feeling. Are they energized or tired? Do they feel satisfied or frustrated? Ask for their suggestions to perk things up.

Process checks can also be done in written form by posting an exit survey on a flipchart near the door. Members can then anonymously rate how the meeting is going thus far. When members return from the break, ask them to interpret the survey results and brainstorm ideas for improving the remainder of the session. Act on their suggestions immediately.

7. Take minutes.
Assign responsibility for taking very brief, concise notes to someone in the group.

8. Determine next steps.
Never let a group leave a meeting without clear next-steps in place. This means defining what will be done, by whom, and when. These action plans need to be brought forward at all subsequent meetings to make sure there is follow-through on commitments.

9. Evaluate the meeting.
Always have the group review and evaluate each meeting. This evaluation should include what can be done to improve the next meeting, as well as feedback for the facilitator.

There are three ways to evaluate a meeting:

- Forcefield Analysis: Ask:

  "What were the strengths of today's meeting?"

  "What were the weaknesses?"

  "What should we do to correct the weaknesses?"

- Exit Survey: Write three to six questions on a sheet of flipchart paper, and post it near an exit. Discuss the results at the start of the next meeting.

Sample Exit Survey

Tell us how it's going so far

Progress: To what extent are we achieving our goals?

1	2	3	4	5
Poor	Fair	Satisfactory	Good	Excellent

Pace: How does the pace feel?

1	2	3	4	5
Far too slow	Slow	Just right	Fast	Far too fast

Process: Are we using the right methods/tools?

1	2	3	4	5
Not at all		Somewhat		Extremely effective

Pulse: How are you feeling about the session?

1	2	3	4	5
Totally frustrated	Exhausted	Satisfied	Pleased	Energized

Additional exit survey questions include:
- Output: To what extent did we achieve what we needed to?
- Time: How well did we use our time?
- Participation: How well did we ensure everyone was equally involved?
- Decision making: How well-thought-out were our decisions?

- Formal Survey: At least once a year, administer a survey of key meeting elements. Discuss the results and look for improvements.

Redesigned Meeting Agenda Worksheet

(180 minutes)

Agenda Items and Time	Process Notes
1. Welcome, Agenda Overview, and Agenda Ratification (10 min.)	Gain buy-in to the agenda. Multi-vote time allocations and agenda order. Finalize meeting priorities and flow.
2. Establish Norms (15 min.)	Ask members to think back to the last meeting. Ask for suggestions for rules that will make this meeting better. Post these rules.
3.	
4.	
Break (15 min.)	
5.	
6.	
7. Agenda for the Next Meeting (10 min.)	Members collaborate to suggest items for the next meeting. Proposed items are posted for prioritization.
8. Adjournment	As members exit, they vote to rank the next meeting's agenda items and also share observations on the exit survey.

Facilitation Dynamics

To get maximum benefit from this module, think about the effectiveness of your office group's meetings and identify strategies that would make future meetings better. Try to think of at least one improvement idea for each ineffective element.

Effective elements ✔	Ineffective elements ✘	Improvement ideas

Take a few minutes to reflect on meeting design and organization.

How can your work group use facilitation to make meetings better?

What are the most significant things you have gained from this training program about facilitation?

What do you still need to learn or do to become even more skilled and confident?

We hope that you've enjoyed this introduction to facilitation. While you now have enough information to begin helping groups, you've probably also realized that there is a lot more to learn!

Consider the following activities as ways to continue your learning journey in this important skill area.

1. Complete the skills self-assessment questionnaire and identify the specific topics you want to spend more time learning about. Consider attending a more advanced training program to develop additional skills.

2. Find a partner who has had facilitation training and ask them to be your coach. Arrange to have them watch you facilitate a meeting and then get their feedback. Remember that observing others is an important way to learn, so plan to also take a turn observing and coaching others.

3. Read more about facilitation. There are a lot of books in bookstores and on the internet.

4. Practice, practice, practice. The only way to learn is to do it so identify facilitation as one of your personal learning objectives. Look for opportunities in your organization to get facilitation assignments in your own and other departments.

Mastering the art of neutrality, keeping notes, and asking questions at meetings is not all there is to facilitating. Being a true facilitator means developing your competency at four distinct levels.

Review the skills needed at each of the four levels described below. Then complete the "Facilitation Skills Self-Assessment" to identify your current strengths and future training needs.

Level 1

Understanding concepts, values, and beliefs; use of facilitative behaviors such as active listening, paraphrasing, questioning, and summarizing; managing time; encouraging participation; keeping clear and accurate notes; using basic tools like problem solving and action planning.

Level 2

Mastering process tools; designing meetings; skilled at using the right decision-making method, achieving consensus, and getting true closure; handling feedback activities and conducting process checks; using exit surveys; managing meetings in an effective manner; helping a group set goals and objectives that are measurable; skilled at checking assumptions and challenging ideas.

Level 3

Skilled at managing conflict and making immediate interventions; able to deal with resistance and personal attacks; making design changes on the spot; sizing up a group and using the right strategies for its developmental stage; managing survey feedback exercises; able to design and conduct interviews and focus groups; designing and implementing surveys; consolidating ideas from a mass of information into coherent summaries.

Level 4

Designing and implementing process interventions in response to complex organizational issues; using tools to promote process improvement, customer intimacy, and overall organizational effectiveness; able to support teams in the various stages of team development.

Facilitation Skills Self-Assessment

Assess your current skill levels by rating yourself according to the basic skill areas outlined below. Rate your current skill level on a four-point scale (1 = no skill; 2 = a little skill; 3 = good skill level; and 4 = completely competent).

Level 1
Rating

1. Understand the concepts, values, and beliefs of facilitation. _____
2. Skilled at active listening, paraphrasing, questioning, and summarizing key points. _____
3. Able to manage time and maintain a good pace. _____
4. Armed with techniques for getting active participation and generating ideas. _____
5. Keep clear and accurate notes that reflect what participants have said. _____
6. Familiar with the basic tools of systematic problem solving, brainstorming, and forcefield analysis. _____

Level 2

1. Knowledge of a wide range of procedural tools essential for structuring group discussions. _____
2. Able to design meetings using a broad set of process tools. _____
3. Knowledge of the six decision-making options. _____
4. Skilled at achieving consensus and gaining closure. _____
5. Skilled at using feedback processes and able to accept personal feedback. _____
6. Able to set goals and objectives that are measurable. _____
7. Able to ask good probing questions that challenge assumptions in a nonthreatening way. _____
8. Able to stop the action and check on how things are going. _____
9. Able to use exit surveys to improve performance. _____
10. Able to manage meetings in an orderly and effective manner. _____

Level 3

1. Able to manage conflict between participants and remain composed. _____
2. Able to make quick and effective interventions. _____
3. Able to deal with resistance non-defensively. _____
4. Skilled at dealing with personal attacks. _____
5. Able to redesign meeting processes on the spot. _____
6. Able to size up a group and use the right strategies for their developmental stage. _____
7. Able to implement survey feedback exercises. _____
8. Able to design and conduct interviews and focus groups. _____
9. Knowledgeable about survey design and questionnaire development. _____
10. Able to integrate and consolidate ideas from a mass of information and create coherent summaries. _____

Level 4   Rating

1. Able to design and implement process interventions in response to complex   _____
   organizational issues.
2. Able to facilitate process improvement, customer intimacy, and other organizational   _____
   development activities.
3. Able to support teams in their forming, storming, and performing stages.   _____

My current skills (Include all the items you ranked as 3 or 4):

_____

_____

_____

_____

The skills I most need to work on (Choose the ones most immediately important from all the items
ranked as 1 or 2):

_____

_____

_____

_____

Improving the Way Organizations Run

GOAL/QPC is a leading, worldwide provider of information, tools, and services for organizational improvement. We are a not-for-profit research, publishing, and training company dedicated to helping people achieve performance excellence.

Our best-selling product line, The Memory Jogger™ series, is designed to give everyone in the organization the tools and methods for organizational improvement. We also provide off-the-shelf training materials, software, books, videotapes, and training courses to help you meet your improvement goals.

Visit our web site today and learn how people around the world, in all types of organizations and industries, use our materials for:

- Process Management and Improvement
- Problem Solving
- Project Management
- ISO 9001:2000 Compliance
- Strategic Planning
- Team Facilitation and Coaching
- Customer Focus
- Innovation and Creativity
- Six Sigma
- Lean Enterprise

Toll Free: 800-643-4316
Sales Direct: 603-893-1944 • Fax: 603-870-9122
service@goalqpc.com • www.goalqpc.com